Seasonal Cycles

WRITTEN BY
Nadia Mike

There are five seasons
in Nunavut.

There is winter, early spring, spring, summer, and fall.

It is very cold in winter.
The sea ice freezes.

The days become very short.

The days become longer
in early spring.

The weather is warmer in spring.
The snow starts to melt.

The weather is warm in summer. The ice breaks up.

The days are long. Sometimes
there is no darkness.

It starts to get cooler in fall.
Ice and frost start to form.

It becomes darker
earlier each day.

These are the five
seasons in Nunavut.